science

Shirley Clarke & Barry Silsby

Illustrated by Karen Constantine

Brockhampton Press
LONDON

NOTES FOR PARENTS

Research has shown that when children and parents work together at home, the child's work at school improves.

The purpose of the *Headstart* books is to provide activities which your child will enjoy doing and which will encourage learning to take place in the home.

You can help your child get the most out of this book by:

- *giving help* where necessary (for example, by reading instructions, helping to fill in a table);
- *reading the advice below.* This gives further information and explains the purpose of each activity;
- *talking* to your child about an activity, to encourage him or her to put thoughts into words;
- *encouraging* your child to be a 'scientist' (by asking why and how things happen and trying to think of ways to find out);
- *showing enthusiasm* and interest in your child's involvement in the book. (Confidence grows with adult approval.)

Pages 4–5 Same or different

The purpose of this is to look at similarities as well as differences between people. Some children will be satisfied with ticking whether height, for example, is the same or different, whereas others might want to measure. This activity can give rise to much useful discussion (for example, 'Why do our voices sound different?').

Pages 6–7 Growing experiment
The beans should be ready to measure after two weeks, but as growing conditions vary, it might be necessary to vary the timing. Your child will probably need help if he or she chooses to transplant the beans. Potting compost is best for indoors, although garden soil can be used. The root and bean should be inserted into a hole in the compost/soil, with the stalk showing above, and then firmed in. Don't forget to talk to your child about regular watering and putting the bean in a light place if planted indoors.

Pages 8–9 Seasons

Your child might need to discuss with you the changes brought about by seasons. You should encourage your child to think of events (for example, a summer holiday) to remind him or her of weather conditions, clothes worn, etc.

Pages 14–15 Magnet experiment

Your child might need help to decide what material objects are made from (for example, wood or metal). There is provision for objects made of more than one thing ('Magnet sticks to some of it'). For example, the magnet is attracted to the metal point of a pen, but not the plastic barrel.

Pages 10–11 Ramp experiment

This can be done in various ways. For example, the vehicle which goes the furthest could be recorded by position (first, second, etc.) or distance. Similarly, the reason for a vehicle going the furthest has been left deliberately open, as children should express their own ideas about their reasons. This will help them become enquiring scientists, who will want to know why things happen and later test them out.

Pages 18–19 Light experiment

The idea of this is to show that different materials let different amounts of light through. Although the picture and examples are of fabric type materials, your child might be interested in trying other types of materials, such as wood, glass, china, etc. Try encouraging your child to predict whether the light will shine through or not *before* switching on the torch.

Pages 12–13 Baby hunt

Your child might need to look hard for the difference between a duckling or a chick (feet, bill), or may need to explain to you about the connection between a butterfly and caterpillar, or a frog and a tadpole.

Pages 22–3 What do I need?

Some objects are obvious, for example, soap to keep clean, whereas others depend on the child. (Some might need a soft toy to help them sleep, others might not.) There is room for a great deal of discussion about a healthy life style on this page.

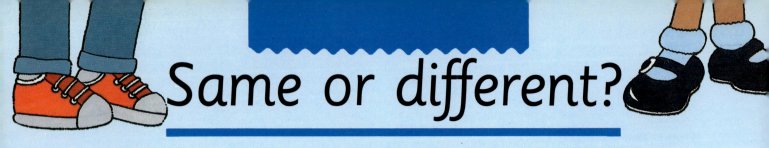

Same or different?

Draw a picture of you in the first box.

Draw a picture of someone else from your family in the second box.

My name ....

Her/his name ....

Look at how the two of you are the same and how you are different.

Put a ✓ for same and an ✗ for different.

	Same (✓) or different (✗)?
Age	
Sex	
Hair colour	
Hair style	
Skin colour	
Eye colour	
Height	
Weight	
Shoe size	
Sound of voice	
.... Write one of your own ideas here.	

Are you more similar or less similar?

More	
Less	

Growing experiment

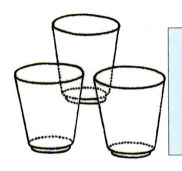

You need

3 glasses

3 runner beans
(from a seed packet)

3 pieces of kitchen paper

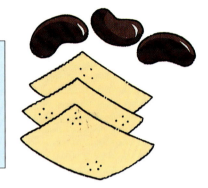

Fold the pieces of kitchen paper and line the glasses with them.

Pour about 2 cm of water into the bottom of each glass.

Push a bean between the paper and the wall of the glass.
(Make sure it is *above* the water level.)

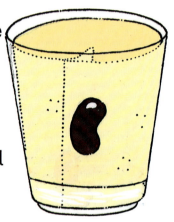

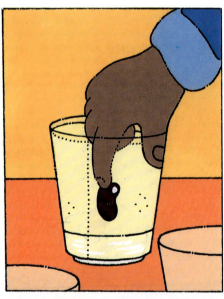

Put the glasses on a windowsill in a warm room and look at them every day.

	Bean 1	Bean 2	Bean 3
How many days did the root take to appear?			
How many days did the leaf take to appear?			
How many days did the stalk take to appear?			
After two weeks, measure the beans.			

Which bean grew best? ....

This is a good way to start bean plants.

In Spring or Summer you could plant them in the garden.

At other times, you could plant them in a flower pot and keep them indoors.

They will need a stick to climb up.

Seasons

Look carefully at this Winter picture.

How would it be different if it was Summer?

Clues

trees

flower beds

Can you finish this picture to make it Summer?

sky

wildlife

clothes

Ramp experiment

You need

- Some toy vehicles
- A piece of card or wood to make a ramp
- A box

Make a ramp like this.

Which of your toy vehicles will travel the furthest if you let them go down the ramp?

Test each one more than once to make sure.

My toys	First go	Second go	Third go

My ………………………………… was the best vehicle because

…………………………………………………………………………………………… .

……………………………………………………………………………………………

Baby hunt

Help the mothers find their babies.
Join them with a line.

Magnet experiment

You need

A magnet

Use your magnet in the house to see which things it will stick to (is attracted to).

Do you know what each object is made of?
Ask an older brother or sister, or an adult.
Fill in the table opposite.

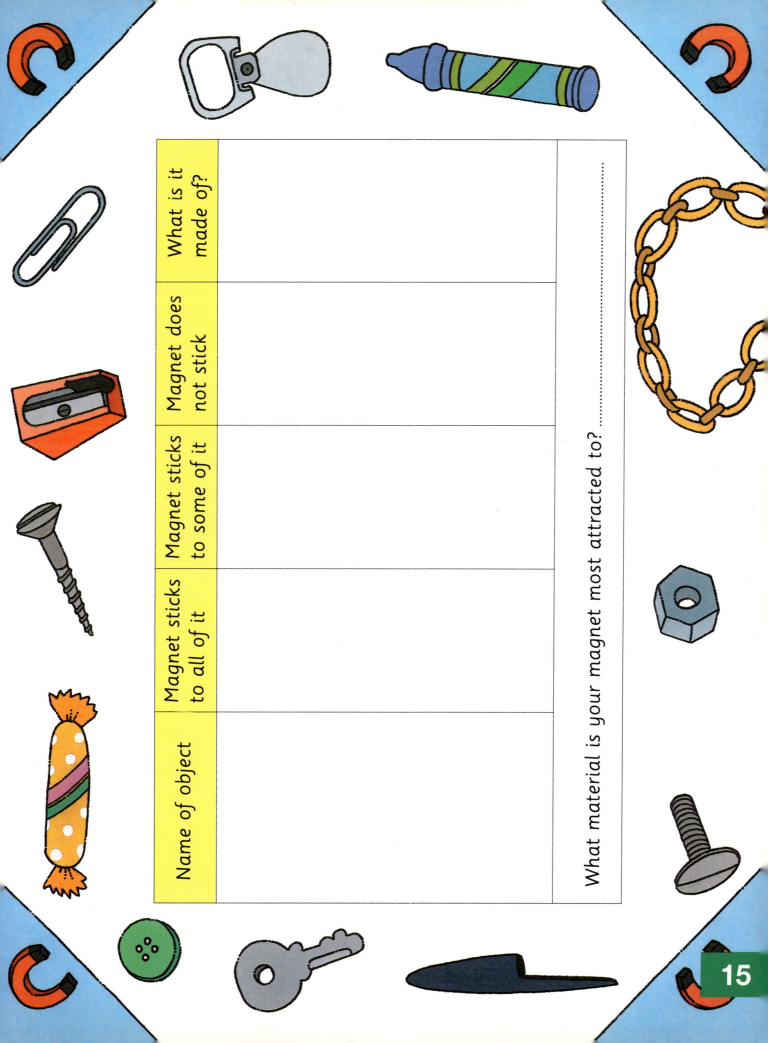

Name of object	Magnet sticks to all of it	Magnet sticks to some of it	Magnet does not stick	What is it made of?

What material is your magnet most attracted to? ....

Danger!

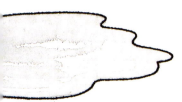

Draw a cross wherever you can see danger in the kitchen.

Can you say why each is dangerous?

(Answers on page 24.)

Light experiment

You need
- A torch
- Some pieces of material

Put a piece of material over your torch.
You could use a handkerchief, a piece of plastic, a tissue or anything else you can think of.

Make sure you only have one layer.

Now switch the torch on.
Does the light shine through the material or not?

Do the same with lots of different types of materials and fill out the table on the next page.

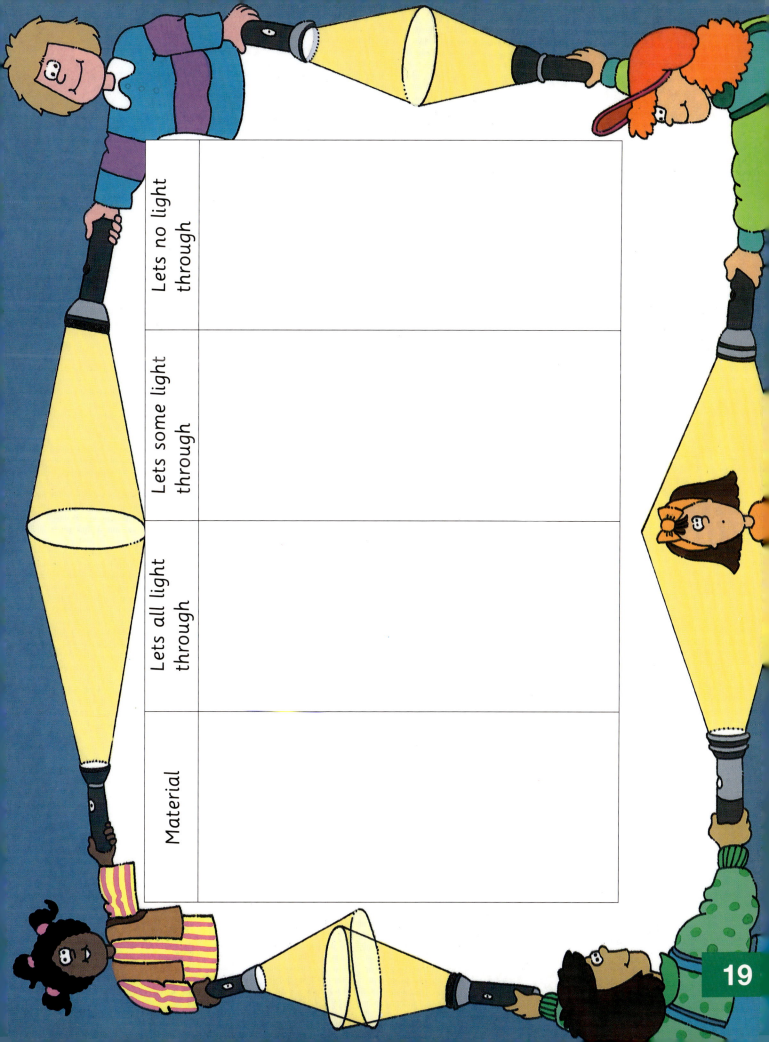

Weather

These are some of the symbols used to show what the weather will be like.

cloudy   sun and cloud   stormy

sunny   rainy   foggy

Watch TV to see what other symbols are used.

Look at the map on the next page.
Be a weather forecaster!

In Scotland it will be

....

In England it will be

....

In Wales it will be

....

In Ireland it will be

....

What do I need?

Put a ring around all the things you need.

What do I need to keep me clean?

What do I need to give me energy?

What do I need to keep fit?

What do I need to help me sleep?

ANSWERS TO PAGE 16–17

We can see ten dangers — can you see any more?

1. TV too close to sink — electricity and water don't mix.
2. Trailing wires across floor.
3. Trailing wire from iron is at the right height for the baby to reach and pull the iron down on his or her head.

4 and 5 Electric fire is unguarded AND is too close to the washing.

6. The child should not be balancing like that to reach something too high for her. Either she will fall or she will pull something from the shelf down on her head.
7. Health hazard: all animals carry germs and should not be near food or on food surfaces.
8. Water makes the floor slippery. It should be mopped up immediately it is spilt.
9. Switch off electric rings immediately they are finished with.
10. Saucepan handles should face inwards and never be left sticking out over the side of the cooker.

British Library Cataloguing in Publication Data
Clarke, Shirley
  Headstart: science: 5-7. – (Headstart)
  I. Title II. Silsby, Barry III. Series
  372.3

ISBN 1-86019-522-9

This edition published 1997 by Brockhampton Press, a member of Hodder Headline PLC Group.
10 9 8 7 6 5 4 3 2
1999 1998 1997

© 1992 Shirley Clarke and Barry Silsby

All rights reserved. No part of this publication may be reproduced or transmitted in any form or by any means, electronic or mechanical, including photocopy, recording, or any information storage and retrieval system, without permission in writing from the publisher or under licence from the Copyright Licensing Agency Limited. Further details of such licences (for reprographic reproduction) may be obtained from the Copyright Licensing Agency Limited, of 90 Tottenham Court Road, London W1P 9HE.

Typeset by Oxprint, Oxford OX2 6TR
Printed in India.